Joseph Jastrow

Belief
and
Credulity

For general information on our products and services, please contact us on prodinnova@mail.com

Printed in United States.

ISBN : 978-1532970467

10 9 8 7 6 5 4 3 2 1

Joseph Jastrow

Belief
and
Credulity

Contents

Chapter I

The vital history of human development is to be sought in the history of beliefs. The inscriptions of Egypt or of Babylon, tho rendered in modern tongues, speak an imperfect message until illuminated by some insight into the beliefs which these cultures cherished. The amazing ruins of Copan, the serpent mound of Ohio, remain mute and inglorious until we can solve the riddle of the beliefs of their builders. Dead Pompeii becomes a living city when we people its streets with the hopes and fears, the beliefs and opinions of its last inhabitants. The history of the arts and the sciences, of society and of religion, specifically involves an account of the succession of beliefs and of the growth of belief-habits. The story of men's doings is likewise, in large measure, a reflection of their beliefs; conduct, whether of individuals or of masses of men, remains an undeciphered record until interpreted as the concrete expression of definite beliefs. The spring of action is motive, and the intellectual impetus to motive is again, belief.

Of the outward and of the inward marks of the stages of learning none are more notable than the beliefs which as the result of such learning come to be accepted and promulgated, and the attitude of inclination or disinclination which such beliefs foster in regard to the various and ever-enlarging problems which engage the interests of men. The possession of certain beliefs and a definite belief-attitude differentiates the educated from the uneducated, the scholar from the dilettante, the expert from the layman, the modern spirit from the mediaeval, the traits of this generation from those of its immediate predecessors. For those who would search out the motives and the justifications of their beliefs, it is of constant importance to realize the more potent and the more patent tendencies and influences by which are shaped the opinions alike of the many and of the few; to consider the characteristics which give to certain beliefs and belief-attitudes their logical cogency, their ethical worth, and their social power, and deprive other classes of beliefs from any possible participation in these desiderata. Such an inquiry naturally includes an outlook upon the regions of unwarranted belief, of error and prejudice and credulity.

Joseph Jastrow

A most attractive approach to the problem thus suggested may be found in a remarkable essay by Mr. C. S. Peirce.[1] Belief is there presented as a mental trait possessing and developed by plain advantages of an evolutionary or adaptively useful kind. Such at least would be the case for all simple and practical matters upon which the incipient rationality of primitive man probably cut its teeth. Logicality, Mr. Peirce tells us—and by that is meant a habit of mind that leads to the detection of truth, to thinking about things as they are, to bringing our thoughts into agreement with reality—"logicality in regard to practical matters is the most useful quality an animal can possess, and might, therefore, result from the action of natural selection; but outside of these it is probably of more advantage to the animal to have his mind filled with pleasing and encouraging visions, independently of their truth; and thus, upon unpractical subjects, natural selection might occasion a fallacious tendency of thought." Natural selection certainly has not interfered with the maintenance of untrue and illogical beliefs; and while we may admit some truthward tendency as part of the natural endowments of *homo sapiens*, that tendency by no means dominates his mental habits. Indeed, it is brought to its fruitage only after so much struggle and the learning of so many hard lessons of experience and the slow accumulations of ages of thinking, that it may be appropriately described as an artificial, weakly possessed, and imperfectly disseminated acquisition. We must also remember that practicality, like much else, is a matter of degree; groups of ideas and ways of thinking are more or less practical, and influence action more or less indirectly and by variously roundabout paths; and as the range of human thought widens and diversifies, deepens and becomes more complex, an ever-enlarging circle of human interests and concerns comes to be of this indirectly practical kind. Precept and practice, instead of being connected by a short and straight, stout cord, are no less effectively brought into mutual bondage by a complicated network of strands, many of them delicate in texture, elaborate in weave, and difficult to trace. For present-day purposes we may consider belief as characteristically of this type—complex in structure, subject to endlessly varying influences, modifiable by diverse factors

---

1 "The fixation of belief," *Popular science monthly*, November, 1877.

and circumstances, responsive to social, hereditary, educational, and transitory as well as to more permanent, natural, and logical influences.

A prominent result and indeed a purpose of belief is the concordant settlement of opinion. Yet this result may be brought about—has often been brought about—by other than logical processes; or, speaking with reference to the experience of history, it may be said that it proceeds by methods which are condemned by the most approved logical (and ethical) sanctions of more advanced stages of knowledge, tho it receives the indorsement of the cruder and less enlightened logic of the period. For every work of science—and something analogous is true of reformatory movements in other directions—"great enough to be remembered for a few generations, affords some exemplification of the defective state of the art of reasoning of the time when it was written; and each chief step in science has been a lesson in logic" (Peirce). Of distinctive methods of fixing belief Mr. Peirce describes four: the method of tenacity, of authority, of inclination, of scientific verifiability. The first, when stated baldly, seems devoid of all merit; yet it expresses in extreme form a tendency which the student of belief is certain to encounter. The man of tenacity proceeds upon a faith that the opinion which he holds is the truth, that it is his duty to affirm this conviction, to reiterate it and to cherish it, to refrain from entertaining any considerations which may tend to shake the belief, and to seek all the influences that may strengthen it. Naturally this does not remain a coldly intellectual process, but becomes suffused with an emotional intensity which leads the devotee to look with pity or contempt or horror upon any contrary opinion; even to scorn "weak and illusive reason," and to take refuge in the calm satisfaction of a firm and immutable faith. "When an ostrich buries its head in the sand as danger approaches, it very likely takes the happiest course. It hides the danger and then calmly says there is no danger; and if it feels perfectly sure there is none, why should it raise its head to see?" (Peirce.)

Such an attitude is possible only to an intellectual recluse and, to be consistently maintained, must be kept remote from earthly realities. Even when reserved for non-practical considerations, it breaks down under the social impulse; man was not meant to live alone and neither feels, acts, nor thinks alone. A common influence is necessary to fix men's beliefs alike, and the most expeditious method of producing a consensus of opinion has proved to be that of imposed authority. History is too full of the triumphs and the failures of this method—both equally sad to contemplate—to make it necessary to bring forward illustrations of its procedure. Dogma and manifesto, the trial for heresy and the Index Expurgatorius, the Inquisition and the stake, scholasticism and pedantry, the literalism of the expounders of the Scriptures or of the commentators of Aristotle, the refusal of the orthodox to look thru the telescope to see what they had no authority for observing, or the *E pur si muove* of Galileo—bring to mind realistically the heroic scenes of the dramas for which the method of authority furnishes the common plot. The limitations of this method are certain to be irritatingly felt by the few, however lightly tolerated by the many. The saving remnant that enjoys a wider outlook, and penetrates the mist with which dogma has enveloped the atmosphere, realizes that infallibility is theoretically an idle dream, and practically an artificial fiction: and in so far as others use their eyes and look in forbidden places, they observe that many of the beliefs of men do not fall under the shadow of the pronunciamento, but thrive in the sunshine of common sense. And if this be true of some opinions, why not of others? Unless doubt and questioning and inquiry on all subjects be utterly suppressed, the error of authority will be suspected, the means whereby a sounder belief may be discovered will be at least dimly realized, and some resort to other methods of shaping belief be attempted.

But even when freed from the fetters imposed by authority, the minds of the leaders of men have not always followed in the footsteps of wisdom. They have been prone to overlook the tyranny of their own organization and inheritance, and have come to accept a more liberal and humane dictator and one of their own seeking—but a dictator none the less. They believed what was agreeable to reason; they accepted that to which they naturally inclined; and the philosophers of cultivation inclined to beliefs that were plausible, or comforting, or stimulating, or uplifting, or liberalizing. Congenial spirits found one another or a common leader, and schools of opinion came and went. The pendulum swung now this way and now that; here a dominant leader impressed his personality strongly upon his contemporaries; there a reaction from an extreme doctrine induced attention to new lines of thought; everywhere opinion came to be more responsive to influences from without—from practice and experience, from custom and institution. But whatever progress results under this régime is fitful, and hazardous, and ill-defined; it is only when the causes of our inclination are scrutinized and the objective worth, not the agreeableness, of our reasoning comes to be regarded as of primary import, that the pursuit of knowledge, and the fixation of belief in which it results, realize their allegiance to a higher power. Strange gods have been worshiped in strange ways by the followers of their inclinations; the intuitionalists and the mystics and those who believed themselves inspired—tho the inspiration of one was folly and anathema to another—have therein found exercise for their inalienable right to liberty and the pursuit of happiness. "Truth," Lowell explains, "is said to lie at the bottom of a well for the very reason, perhaps, that whoever looks down in search of her sees his own image at the bottom, and is persuaded not only that he has seen the goddess, but that she is far better-looking than he had imagined."

The method of scientific verification has been so wrought into the fiber of our thinking that we find it difficult to realize the power and dominion of other sovereigns; we the scientifically minded are the Hellenes, and the others are the *barbaroi*. And rightly so; for the credentials of our sovereignty are the rewards of generations of patient study of the ways of nature, sanctioned by the logical anticipation of natural events, by the practical utilization of natural principles, by a conscientious, impartial, and objective analysis of our own mental processes. For the scepter in the hands of science is neither a symbol of wanton authority, nor a badge of unearned privilege, nor a license for extravagance and caprice, but an emblem of law and order—safeguarding to all the most cherished opportunities for right knowledge, right beliefs, and right actions, in what measure each is wise enough to consent to be thus governed. It is the prerogative of the scientific method that it enthrones the logical right—the true—as the moral law within enthrones the ethical right—the good. The crowning

Joseph Jastrow

virtue becomes not conviction, nor the approval of authority, nor acceptability, nor general credence, but provability. The adoption of this as our sovereign method alters our ideals, even where it modifies but little our practices; it radically transforms our belief-attitude and our outlook, even tho we cannot as yet apply the one nor enter into possession of the other.

Yet we must not complacently assume that the advantages are exclusively incorporated with the one method, or that its adoption is unencumbered with conflict and sacrifice. We shall continue to feel the natural proneness to shape our beliefs by other and less strenuous standards; we are unwilling to, and we need not, abate our appreciation of what the other methods have accomplished in the trials and tribulations of the past. We cannot lightly shake off the tenacity of our convictions, however obtained, nor the inertia that easily, and the incapacity that necessarily, appeals to authority; we shall continue to yearn to believe what is agreeable and to resist unpleasant truths; we may still reserve some corner of our belief-chamber which shall be exempt from the intrusion of inquiry; but, on the whole, however we may defend these tendencies, or apologize for them, or struggle against them, we make some decent attempt to clothe them with the semblance of plausibility and to present them garbed in fashion scientific. "Yes," Mr. Peirce admits, "the other methods do have their merits: a clear logical conscience costs something—just as any virtue, just as all that we cherish, costs us dear. But we should not desire it to be otherwise. The genius of a man's logical method should be loved and reverenced as his bride, whom he has chosen from all the world. He need not condemn the others; on the contrary he may honor them deeply, and in so doing he only honors her the more. But she is the one that he has chosen, and he knows that he was right in making that choice. And having made it, he will work and fight for her, and will not complain that there are blows to take, hoping that there may be as many and as hard to give, and will strive to be the worthy knight and champion of her from the blaze of whose splendors he draws his inspiration and his courage."

From this survey of the methods by which opinion comes to be established and disseminated, we emerge with an appreciation of how it arises that the history of belief—not unlike history in general—is an affair of war and peace; that it deals, on the one hand, with the accounts of the warfare of the scientific method with its rivals, and, on the other, with the internal development, the institutional absorption, and the colonization of its own spirit among outlying cultures. "Logic," Mr. White reminds us, "is not history. History is full of interferences which have cost the earth dear. Strangest of all, some of the direst of them have been made by the best of men, actuated by the purest of motives, and seeking the noblest results." And in the same strain Mr. Morley: "It is surely the midsummer madness of philosophic complacency to think that we have come by the shortest and easiest of all imaginable routes to our present point in the march; to suppose that we have wasted nothing, lost nothing, cruelly destroyed nothing on the road." "Benevolent assimilation" has always been, as it still appears to be, a difficult art.

From a consideration of the principles by which belief may be rightly and rationally fixed, we proceed to a contemplation of these principles in action. Counsel may be wise, but not practical. We know that the actual formation of true belief is beset with serious difficulties; that the process is likely to be a response to a condition of affairs rather than to a statement of theory. Yet, tho it be a condition and not a theory that confronts us, a knowledge of the theory may be the most effective armament for meeting the condition. If knowledge is power it is as much because method is better than shift as that acquaintance with fact is better than ignorance. Now that science has entered into her kingdom and the vastness of her domain is willingly recognized,—for in a vital sense all that may be known by human ken, supported by evidence, presented in orderly arrangement, related to other knowledge, and developed by further study may be called science,—the busy problem is the infusion of the scientific method into all our ways of thinking, its application to all the various kinds of beliefs that affect our ideals, our working conceptions, and our actions. In so far as this is accomplished there is developed a scientific-mindedness, a rationality and symmetry of judgment, which shall give to the conception of what is possible and what impossible, what probable and what improbable, what established and what disproved, a maximum of clearness, soundness, accuracy, and practicality. It is

Joseph Jastrow

this habit of mind that makes one keen-scented for right beliefs and secure, not from error indeed, but from rash credulity.

It would be most unscientific to overlook the fact that many departments of human interest are not ready for—and in their nature may not be readily subject to—the concrete and exact application of the scientific method. But this recognition offers no excuse for removing such classes of beliefs from the influence of the rationalizing spirit and of the same scientific habits of mind that have created such a beneficent and stimulating atmosphere in more exact realms of thought. Such an influence results in what may be termed a belief-attitude; and this in turn is reflected in one's standards of evidence, contributes to one's expertness of judgment, determines one's inclination or the will to believe, and at the same time gives rise to diversity among the opinions of the wisest as well as to the more glaring disagreements of all sorts and conditions of minds. But when we are in accord in regard to a general fundamental method, such diversities are not to be feared. What Mr. Morley aptly notes of personal companionship—that its painful element is not difference of opinion, but discord of temperament—is equally apposite of intellectual pursuits in general. "Harmony of aim, not identity of conclusion, is the secret of the sympathetic life." Such differences of opinion fall within the range of valid beliefs; those that do not—and many of them fall beyond the pale because of their discord of temperament, their alliance with other methods of fixing belief—may be variously characterized as error, fallacy, superstition, extravagance; and for the habits of mind that tend to the acceptance of false beliefs the terms illogicality and credulity are apposite. The former is commonly understood as referring to the proneness when confronted with the premises to draw false conclusions therefrom; the latter as a too great readiness to accept the premises on insufficient evidence. Yet in practice they are often found as close companions and appear at the summons of prejudice, ignorance, inertia, and of that weakness of judgment and vacillation of standards of belief that flourish, weed-like, when the scientific habit of mind is not assiduously cultivated.

It is important to illustrate that the forces that have been most productive of error in the past are not wholly shorn of their strength in the present; that these tendencies to act upon data credulously, with perverted logic and distorted evidence, however different the fashion of the garments in which they are paraded, are still recognizably the same persistent human frailties that detract from the complete appropriateness of the definition of man as a rational animal. It is further to be noted that quite too many of these misdemeanors are laid to the charge of ignorance; in truth ignorance cannot usually prove an alibi, but it remains to discover the influences that prevented the dispelling of the ignorance, and therein will be found the *vera causa* of the credulity. Mr. Lecky reminds those who would investigate the causes of existing beliefs that a change of opinion is apt to imply, more than anything else, a change in the habits of thinking. "Definite arguments are the symptoms and pretexts, but seldom the causes of the change." "Reasoning which in one age would make no impression whatever, in the next age is received with enthusiastic applause." As we travel in retrospect along the stepping-stones from myth to science, from credulity to logicality, we find rather little disproof and very much outgrowth.[2] It is because we have a more appropriate, that is, a truer way of regarding a certain cluster of phenomena, that we discard the old way; and this truer conception, reached partly by new fact, partly by new argument, partly by new insight, partly by new applications of method, is the logical legacy which the successive "heirs of all the ages"— each in turn "in the foremost ranks of time"—bequeath to their descendants.

The word-learning of the scholastics is reflected in their explanation of the existence of fossils by recourse to a "stone-making force," or

---

2 What Dr. Holmes observes of the homeopathic extravagances is characteristically true of many another error. "Were all the hospital physicians of Europe and America to devote themselves, for the requisite period, to this sole pursuit, and were their results to he unanimous as to the total worthlessness of the whole system in practice, this slippery delusion would slide thru their fingers without the slightest discomposure, when, as they supposed, they had crushed every joint in its tortuous and trailing body." "Many an error of thought and learning has fallen before such a gradual growth of thoughtful and learned opposition. But such things as the quadrature of the circle, etc., are never put down. And why? Because thought can influence thought, but thought cannot influence self-conceit; learning can annihilate learning, but learning cannot annihilate ignorance. A sword may cut thru an iron bar, and the severed ends will not unite; let it go thru the air, and the yielding substance is whole again in a moment" (De Morgan).

Joseph Jastrow

a "lapidific juice," or a "seminal air," or a "tumultuous movement of terrestrial exhalations"; the theologizing proclivities of the upholders of scriptural literalism appear in their accounting for fossils as "sports of nature," as models made by the Creator before he had decided upon the most suitable forms for the animals to assume, or as snares hidden by the Almighty to tempt the unorthodox. Voltaire argued that "fossil fishes were the remains of fishes intended for food, but spoiled and thrown away by travelers; that the fossil shells were accidentally dropped by Crusaders and pilgrims returning from the Holy Land," and one Beringer indited ponderous tomes to prove that they were "stones of a peculiar sort, hidden by the Author of nature for his own pleasure." Beringer's work deserves a prominent place in the museum of credulity; for it is related that some of his mischievous students prepared baked-clay fossils of fish, flesh, and fowl, most fearfully and wonderfully made—and even specimens with Hebrew and Syriac inscriptions upon them—and buried them in the professor's favorite digging places. Illustrations of the miraculous fossils appear on the plates of his curious work,[3] which the author was very zealous in suppressing when the deception became known; but what was the fate of the students history telleth not. Now these fossil views seem to us not merely disproved, but absurd; not merely weakly supported, but distorted. We cannot without serious effort assume the point of view under which they might be considered as remotely plausible. The prepossessions that opened men's ears to such hypotheses are not only foreign to present-day conceptions, but—and this has been frequently overlooked—are antagonistic to the essential spirit of scientific verifiability. The philosophers to whom Charles II. propounded his problem—why a bowl filled with water to the brim would not overflow when a live fish was put into it—were not merely credulous, but were innocent of the habit of thinking that resorts promptly and naturally to verification. It is not easy to reach a decision in regard to the erroneous views of the past, as to how far prepossession blinded men to actual evidence, how far decisive facts were not available, how far logical methods were weakly handled; each of these was frequently present and acted

---

3 The *affaire* Beringer is described in White, *A History of the warfare of science with theology*, I: 216.

Chapter I

both as cause and effect. This, however, is deserving of emphasis: that when the method of science is put in the first place, significant facts will be observed and looked for, arguments pro and con will be weighed, the dangers of prepossession will be realized. Not that this will always be done wisely and well, nor that error will necessarily be avoided; but that the steps that are taken, even tho they be small and tentative and meandering, are more likely than on any other method to be in the right direction. Our scales may be crude, our weights only approximate; but even so, the result is more likely to be trustworthy than if we abandon them and resort to guesswork, or, retaining them, put down our own fist on one end of the beam.

It thus seems proper to speak of the combined logical and psychological weaknesses that tend to the acceptance of unreal evidence and of irrelevant explanation as credulity; and the problem of problems, alike in the voyages of discovery and in everyday cruising on waters great and small, is to equip the pilot so that he may steer his course by right belief and not by credulity. The intellectual mariner's compass, for all purposes alike, is the method of science; but none the less pilotage is an art. Many shores are imperfectly charted; there are reefs and shoals, storms and fogs; breakages in the machinery and lack of training in the crew. These are the dangers of the seas—and shipwrecks are not uncommon; but how much more imminent the dangers, and how almost impossible the traffic, without any compass or with a less reliable one! It is the worthy ambition that brightens the hopes of many a scholar to contribute, in what way it may be possible for each, some aid to the extension, the greater availability, the greater convenience and safety of the highways or of the equipment of intellectual navigation.

Chapter II

From what has been presented it might be inferred that the contemplation of error is more instructive than the story of the evolution of truth; and for certain purposes this is really the case. Error and credulity have thus far been utilized as a background against which to set off right belief; it will be useful to examine the background itself. Credulity is most generally exercised in regard to the acceptance of statements by others. When shall we believe what we are told, and when shall we suspect, discredit, deny? Again no golden rule; no automatic switch that makes connection when truth presses the button, but refuses to work for the touch of error; but also again, the possibility of reaching principles that may train the judgment and guide practice. Clifford has formulated these in a simple and acceptable fashion. You may believe another when "there is reasonable ground for supposing that he knows of the matter of which he speaks, and that he is speaking the truth so far as he knows it." A man may deliberately lie; he may belong to the class to which Huxley refers when he speaks of "the downright lying of people whose word it is impossible to doubt"; he may be more or less consciously or subconsciously misled by his imagination; he may be hopelessly deficient in his powers of observation, or in his knowledge of fact, or in his capacity to handle evidence and argument; and none of these ethical or logical shortcomings seems to interfere at all in certain persons with their powers of holding and publishing opinions on all manners of subjects—even on those on which no human soul has the possibility of possessing knowledge. To Clifford's dual conditions of logical responsibility must be added another pair; namely the distinction as to how far the issue involved is a matter of fact or of the interpretation of fact. Both facts and their interpretation, or arguments, appear as prominently on the side of error as of truth; yet, tho not reducible to anthropometric measurements, the physiognomies of the two are recognizably different to the trained observer.

It seems ludicrously easy to collect facts of any desired quality and to point them in any desired direction. Dr. Holmes effectively describes these abuses: "Foremost of all, emblazoned at the head of every column, loudest shouted by every triumphant disputant, held up as paramount to all other considerations, stretched like an impenetrable shield to protect the weakest advocate of the great cause against the weapons of the adversary, was that omnipotent monosyllable which has been the patrimony of cheats and the currency of dupes from time immemorial,—Facts! Facts! Facts!" Yet in the crucible of logic it is possible to separate the dross from the gold. The arguments employed have a like suspicious appearance: they "have been so long bruised and battered round in the cause of every doctrine and pretension, new, monstrous, or deliriously impossible, that each of them is as odiously familiar to the scientific scholar as the faces of so many old acquaintances, among the less reputable classes, to the officers of police." The former type of credulity—the rash acceptance of facts—is the more simple and the more usually considered; the latter type— the rash acceptance of explanations of interpretations of facts—is frequently the more vital and instructive. Ingenious and successful lying is doubtless a fine art: yet the more difficult part of it is the gaining of credence for one's inventions. That depends largely upon the belief-attitude of the public and upon the psychological climate in which they live. It is quite obvious that the conscienceless prevaricator or charlatan must play upon the prejudices and vanities and ignorance and cupidities of his clientèle. He presents what they wish to believe, appeals to their passions and emotional weaknesses, and when necessary berates his opponents with no gentle hand, and indulges in what Huxley speaks of as "varnishing the fair face of truth with that pestilent cosmetic, rhetoric." But the psychologist's interest is predominantly on the other side, with the duped rather than with the knave; especially if it be a case in which contagion has a fair field and all judgment becomes lost in a psychic epidemic of credulity. Such we are apt to associate with dark ages and ignorant communities, with isolated cultures and inhospitable mental climates. A few instances from the days of the telegraph and the omnipresent daily paper may accordingly be the more instructive.[1]

---

1 Dr. Holmes's *Homeopathy and its kindred delusions*, first published about sixty years ago, was substantially a study of credulity as applied to medical matters. Readers of this will recall that besides the minute exposure of the baselessness of the Hahnemannian cult, there are there considered (1) the royal cure of the King's Evil; (2) the Weapon Ointment and the Sympathetic Powder, the first rather lukewarmly considered by Bacon, the latter brought into notoriety by Sir Kenelm Digby; (3) the Tar-water mania of Bishop Berkeley; (4) the history of the Metallic Tractors, or Perkinsism. These are thus summarized: "The *first two* illustrate the ease with which numerous facts are accumulated to prove the most fanciful and senseless extravagances. The *third* exhibits the entire insufficiency of exalted wisdom, immaculate honesty, and vast general acquirements to make a good physician of a great bishop. The *fourth* shows us the intimate machinery of an extinct

Joseph Jastrow

Chapter III

The name of Leo Taxil—a pseudonym for Gabriel Jorgand—may be unknown to many readers; it should not remain so, for the judgment which has been pronounced upon Mme. Blavatsky— also a modern of the moderns—may with modifications be applied to Taxil; that he "has achieved a title to permanent remembrance as one of the most accomplished, ingenious, and interesting impostors in history." Only Taxil's accomplishments were of a rather gross order; his boldness surpassed his ingenuity; and the interest is centered in his deeds rather than in his personality. Like most disciples of Cagliostro, his career was a checkered one. In 1885, at the age of thirty-one, he was engaged upon his *magnum opus*, having already appeared as a violent radical in politics—he is a product of France—a rabid anti-clerical, and the author of a libelous pamphlet on the *Secret amours of Pius IX*. The suggestion for his *chef d'oeuvre* was the encyclical of Leo XIII. (1884) directed against the Freemasons, who with others were placed under the ban as subjects of the realms of Satan. After a full confession of the errors of his former ways, Taxil was received back with rejoicing into the bosom of the Church, and thereupon published four volumes of wholly imaginary revelations, revealing the sacrilegious orgies and devil-worship of the Masonic mysteries. For this he received in person the solemn benediction of the Vatican, as well as the material rewards of the sale of one hundred thousand copies of his work and the honor of its translation into English, German, Italian, and Spanish. If it be stated that the German version omitted the volume on the "Masonic sisters," for the reason that it was not thought proper to outrage the moral sense of the community by recounting "the filthiness of the hellish crew," the character of the work may be surmised. Taxil extended the sphere of influence of his imaginary demonolaters to all parts of the world—even

delusion, which flourished only forty years ago; drawn in all its details, as being a rich and comparatively recent illustration of the pretensions, the arguments, the patronage, by means of which windy errors have long been, and will continue to be, swollen into transient consequence. All display in superfluous abundance the boundless credulity and excitability of mankind upon subjects connected with medicine." The account of Perkins and his Metallic Tractors falls in well with the instances here considered.

from Singapore to Charleston, at which latter point the Masonic Grand Master figures as a Satanic Pope, who has at his disposal a telephone, invented and operated by devils, whereby he puts a girdle round about the earth in forty seconds, and a magic bracelet by which he summons Lucifer at his pleasure. Intoxicated by his success and the credulity of his adherents, Taxil's invention runs riot; and he tells the story of a serpent inditing prophecies on the back of a demon who "in order to marry a Freemason, transformed himself into a young lady, and played the piano, evenings, in the form of a crocodile." Taxil gained confederates in other countries, who contributed to the movement according to their several needs and talents. One of the most interesting figures in the story is the fictitious personage, Diana Vaughan—the *pucelle* of the drama and of its *dénouement*. She was given out to be the descendant of Thomas Vaughan, the seventeenth-century mystic, and the goddess Astarte; her Luciferian origin and principles were shown by her horror of all religious observances, by the devils who attended her, and thru whose aid she made excursions to Mars, where she "rode on Schiaparelli's canals, sailed on the Sea of the Sirens, and strolled among the gigantic inhabitants of the planet." Many remarkable incidents of her curious personality are retailed for the benefit of the believers; while poetic justice is appeased by her final conversion to the Church thru the instrumentality of the spirit of Jeanne d'Arc.

When it became necessary to materialize Diana Vaughan for the benefit of the privileged few and to satisfy the skepticism of others, she was cleverly impersonated by "a bright American girl, employed as a copyist in a Parisian typewriter establishment, who wrote all the letters at Taxil's dictation and received a monthly salary of one hundred and fifty francs for her services." This was hardly a fair appreciation of American talent, considering that the money remitted to Diana Vaughan in ten years amounted to more than half a million francs. In 1896 Taxil was a prominent figure in a great anti-masonic congress held at Trent, where indeed he was treated as a hero and a saint. On April 19, 1897, in Paris, there was held by invitation of Diana Vaughan a highly sensational function, at which it had been announced that the miraculous lady would appear. When the moment arrived, Taxil stepped forward and said: "Reverend Sirs, ladies and gentlemen! you wish to see Diana Vaughan. Look at me! I myself am that lady." Then followed an explicit account of the twelve years of imposture and an impudent expression of thanks to the clergy for the unwitting aid in his deviltries; a forced retreat to a neighboring cafe to escape the vengeance of the crowd; a momentary furore, some discussion pro and con; and then, so far as can be learned, the world wagged on and the story ends.[1] Surely this is a remarkable instance of *fin-de-siècle* credulity, and one that will hardly suffer by comparison with mediaeval superstition. Its importance in the present connection lies in the illustration which it furnishes of what may happen in extreme cases when verifiability and scientific-mindedness are wholly ignored, and the methods that appeal to authority and to prepossessions are allowed to run riot. Then standards of probability, as well as the critical attitude, are wholly absent or hopelessly distorted, and credulity has the open door.

Prepossessions are not always so prominent in the evolution of myths that gain acceptance by preying upon credulity. The presence of an indolent atmosphere and of a sympathetic milieu is all that is necessary. Of this the story of Kaspar Hauser, the "wild boy of Nuremberg," furnishes a fairly modern instance; for the Nestors of our generation may easily remember the interest which his case aroused thruout Europe. The commonly accepted tale made him out as an abandoned child, cruelly confined in a dark cell, cut off from all association except with the monster who gave him his daily bread. He became the classic example of the condition of a human being in the absence of all education; he was heralded as a child of nature, as an example of the innocence of man before the fall, as a realization in the flesh of Rousseau's Émile. It was proposed to adopt him as the child of Europe, and he was actually adopted as a son by the Earl of Stanhope. The interest in his case was maintained by the accounts of his marvelous psychic powers, as also by the speculations as to his origin, which brought slander upon many a noble house. He could see a gnat in a spider's web a long distance off, and after twilight; he could distinguish between a pear and an apple and a plum tree by their odor at a distance at

---

1 The account of Taxil is derived from E. P. Evans, "Survival of mediaeval credulity," *Popular science monthly*, March and April, 1900.

Chapter III

which others could barely see the trees; he was overcome by the exhalations of a graveyard several streets off; he could distinguish metals by their different attractions for his fingers, while the vicinity of a hardware shop brought on convulsions; when examined by a homeopathist, he proved in his own person the truth of homeopathy. As to the speculations as to who he might have been, it is enough to say that the gossips and the scholars were equally busy and, with characteristic Teuton thoroness, a bibliography of nearly three hundred numbers was accumulated, recounting the various versions of the story of Kaspar Hauser. The sifted facts out of which, or in spite of which, the various myths sprouted and flourished, are few and luminous. The boy appeared on the streets of Nuremberg with a letter in his hand, which he had doubtless written, and was put in prison as a helpless wayfarer. The original protocol shows that he walked a mile on that day, recited the Lord's prayer, spoke with dialectical peculiarities, said that he had gone to school, showed his fondness for horses, and admitted that the object of the letter, addressed to a captain of cavalry, was to secure him a post in the service. He seemed to feign simple-mindedness and to avoid answering questions. In the one letter was another purporting to have been written sixteen years previously by the mother of the boy, but obviously a forgery. This started the story to which the Burgomaster gave wings by a proclamation elaborating the "wild boy of nature" theory, and embellishing it with fantastic "details calculated to give verisimilitude to an otherwise improbable tale." Learned ignorance in the person of a Professor Daumer— to whom Kaspar was intrusted for his education—still further distorted the simple facts. Tho at first the boy could not speak (this is Daumer's story) and could only understand those who treated him as an infant, this helpless and untutored babe, after three days, performed on the piano, soon after knitted a stocking, and in four weeks was able to entertain the Burgomaster with an account of his years of solitary confinement. Within a month this worthy, but mentally blind, professor had transformed the wild boy into a model of social elegance, who carried on witty conversations, made graceful allusions to the ancient Romans, and played checkers and chess. The story is too full of detail to be further considered; but enough has been given to show the glaring

Joseph Jastrow

inconsistency of the theory of explanation either with the real facts, which almost no one knew, or even with the alleged facts, which were widely circulated. Kaspar's lot simply chanced to fall in pleasant places, and, by accepting the part which the credulity of his surroundings thrust upon him, he was buoyed into fame and made the subject of a *neugeschichtliche Legende*.[2] It is proper enough to add that the backward stage of a practical psychology seventy years ago alone made possible the acceptance of any such caricature of an untutored child of nature. Doubtless many gave no credence to the tale; but its ready acceptance in almost all circles gives it a permanent place in the history of credulity. In contrast with the *affaire* Taxil, the Kaspar incident appeals more to the intellectual than to the emotional weaknesses, and involves a larger share of misinterpretation of fact; while the lack of proper standards to estimate the improbability of what is given out for fact is glaringly obvious in both cases. This personal characteristic of the duped is often more forcibly described as gullibility.

To complete the collection of types of credulity, we should have an instance in which a system of interpretation of facts— not a mere narrative—in itself startling and contradictory to ordinary experience, gains widespread credence, and that in spite of pronounced inconsistency with verifiable observation and common sense. These conditions are remarkably well satisfied by the recent promulgation of the doctrines of Christian Science. Even in this field of intellectual effort the land of the free and the home of the brave has contributed an article worthy to compete with the foreign product. Eagle-like, this system spreads its wings and soars free from the bonds of sense or earth-bound realities, free from human logic and the errors of mortal mind, free from the material impediments which the Author of nature has inconsiderately set in our paths, free to make things so by thinking them so, free to set method and learning and experience at naught. And surely it calls for braveness of no common order to resist the seductive appeals of eye and ear, to sail steadily on heedless of the calls of the sirens of rationality, convinced at the outset that things cannot be as they are, and refusing the nod of recognition to the plebeian

---

2 The true Kaspar Hauser is disclosed in Antonius von der Linde's *Kaspar Hauser*, 2 vols., 1887.

Chapter III

idols of the ills of flesh. It is not necessary in this connection to recount the beliefs of this system; it is sufficient to point out that when thousands of intelligent persons give practical adherence to, and enroll themselves under the banner of, one who teaches that a bunion would be an adequate cause of insanity, if only we held the same belief about the bunion as we do about congestion of the brain; that smallpox is contagious by reason of the same agencies as make weeping or yawning contagious; that fear may be reflected in the body as fractured bones, just as shame is seen rising to the cheek; that anatomy and physiology and hygiene are the husbandmen of sickness and disease, while the reading of a text-book of Christian Science is equally effective in producing health; or that when a healthy horse takes cold without his blanket, it is on account of the poor creature's knowledge of physiology—then such persons can hardly complain if they are cited as instances of modern credulity.

Chapter IV

Such, then, is the background against which logical belief shines forth with contrasted splendor; such are, admittedly in their extreme form, the results of following after strange gods and deserting the narrow path of strenuous rationality, of critically trained judgment, of adherence to verifiable standards of belief. The tale needs no adornment, and the moral is sufficiently pointed to require no hard blows to drive it home. It will be profitable in continuation to survey, tho perforce briefly, the middle distance, the practical field of compromise and of the necessity for action, in which we must needs travel up hill and down dale and cannot take the level road which we wish were possible, in which we must risk error constantly if we would move at all.

In entering the practical arena the philosopher is indeed insensitive or unobservant who does not become conscious of a decided climatic change. He is probably already familiar with various uncomplimentary remarks concerning his unfitness to assume a due share of the responsibilities of life, from the tribute of Frederick the Great ("If," he said, "I wanted to ruin one of my provinces,

Joseph Jastrow

I would make over its government to the philosophers") to the fashionable jibes against the scholar in politics. There is certainly much exaggeration in the current notions of the incompatibility of the reflective and the directive (perhaps it would be unwise to say the active) temperament; and there is much reason for the claim that the science-molded philosopher may say, "*nous avons changé tout cela.*" Indeed a recent writer has forcibly maintained that the nearest analogue of the man of science is the "so-called man of business, and the chief distinction between the two is that the one deals with the unfamiliar, the other with familiar things."[1] This significant difference was long ago presented by De Morgan as one of the advantages that a logical training secures. "I maintain that logic tends to make the power of reason over the unusual and the unfamiliar more nearly equal to the power over the usual and familiar than it would otherwise be. The second is increased; but the first is almost created." This is but one of the differences in training, interest, thought-habit, and temperament that estrange the scholar from the man of affairs. Yet much of this unfamiliarity is a matter of technique, and as such belongs equally to the arts of life and to the sciences; the ignorance of one another's techniques is no cause for lack of sympathy and comprehension of the aims and efforts of practical and scientific specialists. A further contrast is emphasized by philosophical historians. "In practical life, the wisest and soundest men avoid speculation, and insure success because, by limiting their range, they increase the tenacity by which they grasp events; while in speculative life the course is exactly the reverse, since in that department the greater the range, the greater the command, and the object of the philosopher is to have as large a generalization as possible"—this is Buckle's formulation. "Nothing can be more fatal in politics than a preponderance of the philosophical, or in philosophy than a preponderance of the political spirit," says Lecky. Mr. Fiske, in commenting upon the relations of Huxley and Gladstone (whom Huxley himself spoke of as a "copious shuffler"), says: "One could no more expect a prime minister, as such, to understand Huxley's attitude in presence of a scientific problem, than a deaf-mute to comprehend a symphony of Beethoven."

---

1 F. W. Clarke, *Popular science monthly*, February, 1900.

Chapter IV

And yet these occupations are not mutually exclusive; philosophy and politics are not December and May, and the temperate zone, in which (in theory at least) we pass our existence, is a composite of the two. Indeed, a divorce of theory and practice is disastrous to both parties of the alliance; theory is the more real and vital for its consideration of and adaptation to tangible conditions; and practice is more rational and more liberal, embraces a larger expediency than if responsive only to the *status quo*. Learning dissociated from doing is threatened with the decadence of mere erudition, pedantry and disputation. Exercise is equally good for mind and body; but there is danger of falling in love with the mere mechanism of thought—the absorption in the feeling of one's mental muscles contracting and of plodding in treadmill routine, ever moving, but never advancing. The danger of practice dissociated from principle is that of becoming time-serving, narrow, partisan, short-sighted; it tacks for every wind, loses its bearings, and sacrifices larger for smaller gains. Emerson said of the English some fifty year ago: "They are impious in their skepticism of a theory, but kiss the dust before a fact"; and Emerson's own countrymen are curiously like and curiously unlike the people whose traits he characterizes. Mr. Morley deplores the same tendency from a more modern point of view. He notes the inclination to reply to an advocate of improvement by "some sagacious silliness about recognizing the limits of the practical in politics, and seeing the necessity of adapting theories to facts. As if the fact of taking a broader and wiser view than the common crowd disqualifies a man from knowing what the view of the common crowd happens to be, and from estimating it at the proper value for practical purposes." These various opinions, when judiciously strained, leave a weighty deposit of truth; and they have a direct bearing upon the issues of right and wrong belief. They make it abundantly clear that the relations of right knowing to right doing as urgently demand illumination to-day as when Socrates mystified the Athenian youth by maintaining that no man would willingly do wrong or wittingly hold to error. On the one hand, we are told that for wild speculation and rash credulity the practical man takes the lead, whether it be by subscribing in coin to schemes for extracting gold from sea water, or "backing" the rain-makers or the "Keeley motor"; or in subscribing in faith to the reality of curative mental vibrations, the accounts of signaling with the inhabitants of Mars, the depositing of gray matter in Helen Keller's finger-tips, or to any other of the items of the progress of science with which newspaper paragraphers regale their readers when copy is scarce. On the other hand, the men of books and apparatus are charged with the pursuit of fads, of a contempt for journals and ledgers, of an ignorance of business ways, and an incapacity to deal executively with men and things. The truth is that there are all shades and grades of men in both careers; and the important things to be observed are tendencies and their causes, not individuals and their peculiarities. It is these tendencies that are reflected in opinion and conduct indirectly, and directly in the relations that are entertained and acted upon, of theory to practice.

This relation—between the theoretical and the practical factors in the progress of knowledge—may be pictured as similar to that pertaining between master and dog. The dog runs ahead of the master, takes short excursions on his own account, comes to a turn of the road and wanders hesitatingly about until he detects the direction in which his master turns; then dashes confidently onward with an air of having intended to go that way all along, and probably imagines—and the appearances are in his favor— that he is leading the man. Yet the wise dog does not wander far out of scenting distance, is on the alert for the call of the master, and quickly retraces his steps when he finds that his master has turned the other way. It is doubtless true that the dog may light upon valuable discoveries; and the master will do well to heed any unusual signs of alarm or excitement on the part of his keen-scented companion; and if it happens that the shades of night close in upon him or that his own sight grows dim, he that walks in darkness is fortunate in having so trustworthy a guide. From which we may learn that the formation of belief in practical affairs, while seemingly independent of theory and indeed running ahead of theory for short stretches in a restless striving to enrich experience, is none the less directed by theory, and prospers best when following, tho with judgment and self-reliance, the indications of principles and formulae.

The mutual recognition of the functions of theorist and practitioner

Chapter IV

is one of the desired and not improbable consummations of modern civilization, and upon it depends in considerable measure the practical fate of right and wrong beliefs. It is still pertinent to repeat Buckle's complaint that "a theorist is actually a term of reproach instead of being, as it ought to be, a term of honor; for to theorize is the highest function of genius, and the greatest philosophers must always be the greatest theorists"; yet, in so doing, we may add the condition that the philosophers shall theorize wisely and with appreciation of the actualities of existence, not dogmatically or capriciously. In brief, there is scientific theorizing, as there is scientific practice; belief and credulity, truth and error, economy and waste, profit and loss, are possible in each. Yet in the end, rational progress in belief and practice, tho truly a question of proportion, must take its illumination not diffusely from countless scattered sources, but directly from a central luminous principle. "The devotion to the practical aspect of truth"—to cite again from Mr. Morley—"is in such excess as to make people habitually deny that it can be worth while to formulate an opinion, when it happens at the moment to be incapable of realization for the reason that there is no direct prospect of inducing a sufficient number of persons to share it." "As if the mere possibility of the view being a right one did not obviously entitle it to a discussion." "The evil . . . comes of not seeing the great truth that it is worth while to take pains to find out the best way of doing a given task, even if you have strong grounds for suspecting that it will ultimately be done in a worse way." "It makes all the difference in the world," says Whately, "whether we put Truth in the first place or in the second place." Mr. Morley thus protests against what he calls the House of Commons view of life, which subordinates principle to expediency—which may be unfortunate, but necessary—but in so doing sacrifices the paramount significance of principle—which is both unnecessary and pernicious.

The practical arena wherein truth and error, right and wrong, the better and the worse cause, principle and expediency, are engaged in combat is obviously too complex to admit of ready description or analysis; the few groups of combating influences that have been brought within the field of view occupy but a modest corner of the arena. Other equally important contests are going on at the

Joseph Jastrow

same time; the ethical aspects of belief are nearly as complex as the intellectual, and as worthy of consideration; and people still find an interest in discussing how far truth should be disseminated when it undermines traditional convictions seemingly essential to happiness or even to virtue; how far, in Clifford's words, "Truth is a thing to be shouted from the housetops, not to be whispered over rose-water after dinner, when the ladies are gone away," and how far the dissemination of right belief is itself controlled by considerations of practical as well as of theoretical morality. Philosophers of so opposite a calling as a Harvard psychologist and a Parliamentary leader[2] unite in telling us that, in the last analysis, with regard to disputed questions of a not too practical sort, men do and have a right to believe, at their own risk, that which seems to them most elevating, fitting, satisfying, and rational; that in this process we all follow custom and temperamental impulse, tho we cover our retreat with arguments. Into these enticing ramifications of the central problem of right and wrong belief, however germane to the comprehension of the forces that make for truth and error, it is not feasible at present to enter. The issues in which these various factors—and especially the aspects just presented of the relations of theory to practice—culminate is that of the formation of belief-standards. It is in the common possession of these that the logical man of theory and the logical man of practice should find their sympathetic companionship; and to the appreciation of this underlying requisite for harmonious and profitable intercourse, nothing will contribute more directly and effectively than a comprehension of the relations that do and should exist between the guiding principles of belief and their wise embodiment in conduct. If the leaders of men, leaders of small companies and of large ones, those who are listened to and likewise listen to others, can be induced to absorb somewhat of the spirit and the sensitiveness to real distinctions that result from the successful devotion to the aims of science, the danger of the ready acceptance of false beliefs, the fostering of credulity, would be materially lessened.

In an age when many marvelous things have been accomplished, some of them on the surface as unexpected and as unconnected

---

2 James, *The will to believe*; Balfour, *The foundations of belief.*

with other knowledge, indeed as seemingly contradictory of such knowledge, as the ostensible miracles and startling paradoxes that are paraded as demonstrable truth, it is natural enough that the man in the street should be bewildered and not know what to believe nor whom to believe. Between the Scylla of ignorant and obstinate skepticism and the Charybdis of ignorant and rash credulity, the channel seems perplexingly narrow; nor is it always possible to assume the expertness and disinterestedness of those who offer themselves as pilots. The possibility of seeing one's bones thru the skin seems as remote as the possibility of perpetual motion; telepathy no more wonderful than wireless telegraphy; the predictions of the astrological almanac as credible as the determination by the spectroscope of the physical conditions of other planets; the phrenological faculties as satisfying as the results of the physiological study of brain-localizations; the mental vibrations of the "absent treatment" healer as fairly supported by the results as the therapeutic action of drugs; the presentation of the mathematical triturations and the homeopathic potencies as learned and convincing as the enigmatic formulae and manipulations of the chemist. And yet these resemblances are quite superficial, the analogies of their likeness quite misleading. On the one shore lies the orderly kingdom of rational belief; across the border the chaotic realm of credulity.

Anyone who cares to take the trouble of examining the literature (*sic*) of the propaganda of logical unorthodoxy can readily satisfy himself of the reality and the character of the realm over which credulity holds sway. He will observe the truly unbalanced, the "cranks," those possessed with what has been described as the "unconquerable determination of the human race to believe what it knows is not so," the innocently and naively deluded, the faddists and extremists, the seemingly normal and wholly intelligent. The shades and grades of believers are as pronounced as on the other shore. And yet to the man of sturdy intellectual virtue these distorted, tho not wholly valueless, beliefs offer no temptation. And equally true is it that the logically molded thinker knows that it is useless to demand any ready-made prescription which shall save all men from credulity, not only in extreme cases—which most people do not really fear—but in the intermediate and more

Joseph Jastrow

frequent and actual perplexities of the practical life.

The nature of the antidote which most is worth the seeking it has been the purpose of this essay to set forth. And last as first should it be emphasized that there is in many of the vital and typical problems of knowing and doing, an objectively best method of fixing belief to which we may reasonably approximate in practice. Neither the logical requirements of philosophical thought nor the actualities of the practical life, when rightly interpreted, appear to be seriously antagonistic to—indeed are wholly compatible with— the absorption of the principles rooted in the scientific analysis of belief. This infusion of the blood of science permeates the organic structure of the belief-attitude, and creates a sturdy affinity for right belief and a deep-seated aversion for the intellectual manners that error, attractive to credulity, is apt to bear. In truth this protecting aegis is in some measure an aesthetic trait—a certain intellectual fastidiousness which, as is also true of the ethical life, becomes a potent ally of virtue. And this logical virtue becomes recognizable in the ability to guide action and belief by reference to fundamental principles; it requires the quality of mind that easily holds the impress of an argument, whose beliefs are deep-rooted in the soil of human experience critically interpreted.

When confronted with the noisy demonstrations of some new revolutionary claimant for public favor, the well-bred mind, tho plastic to worthily formative influences, is not easily disturbed in its convictions, nor readily affected by the contagion of popular approval. Even tho unable to explain fully the status of the ambitious aspirant, it does not become panic-stricken and lightly transfer its allegiance, nor madly follow a fashionable prestige, however brilliantly heralded. Rather is comfort sought in the reflection that often before have meteors flashed across the sky and disappeared, and still the stars shine fixedly. Across a gap of twenty centuries it finds the touch of nature that renders the whole world kin, and repeats approvingly the sentiment of Lucian: "To defend one's mind against these follies a man must have an adamantine faith, so that, even if he is not able to detect the precise trick by which the illusion is produced, he at any rate retains his conviction that the whole thing is a lie and an impossibility." Such a man knows full well that the baser metals cannot be converted into gold; and

Chapter IV

tho at credulity's

> "booth are all things sold,
> Each ounce of dross costs its ounce of gold,"

he realizes, too, the potent reality of truth; that truth is neither a metaphysical abstraction nor a matter of taste, and least of all a matter of expediency. While judiciously responsive to the practical demands of the conditions under which belief must be wrought out and expressed, he is assured with Lowell that "compromise makes a good umbrella, but a poor roof"; while sympathetic with the more ultimate discussion of the belief process, he holds clearly in mind the functional utility and categorical imperative of right belief. *Das Wahre fördert.*

JOSEPH JASTROW
UNIVERSITY OF WISCONSIN

ISBN : 978-1532970467

www.ingramcontent.com/pod-product-compliance
Lightning Source LLC
Chambersburg PA
CBHW062031280526
45787CB00005B/2280